BLUE RIBBON SERIES
FAVORITE PIANO DUETS
for two players at one piano

PREFACE

These FAVORITE PIANO DUETS are favorites of students and teachers and listeners. The pieces were written by highly respected twentieth-century composers who have specialized in creating music for piano students.

The duets were carefully chosen to insure that each piece is <u>interesting</u> for both players, with the secondo having full partnership with the primo!

CONTENTS

Design: Odalis Soto
Photography: Ron Olman
Piano Courtesy of Morgan Music Company, Miami, Florida
Editor: Carole Flatau

HUNGARIAN DANCE

Secondo

ROGER GROVE

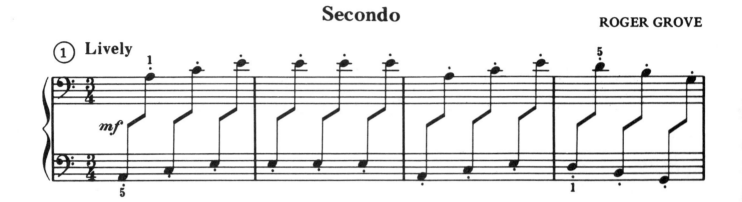

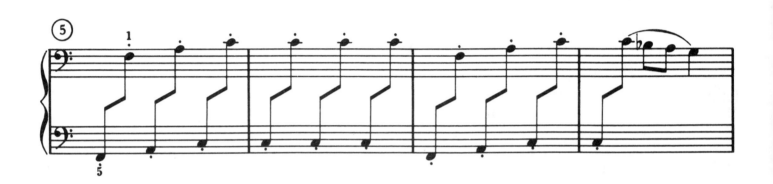

HUNGARIAN DANCE

Primo

ROGER GROVE

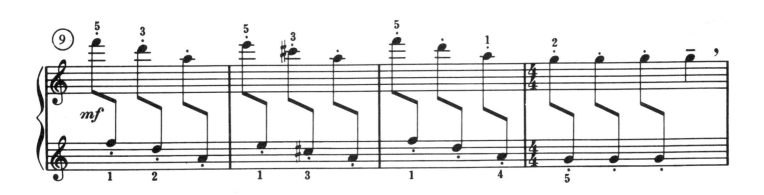

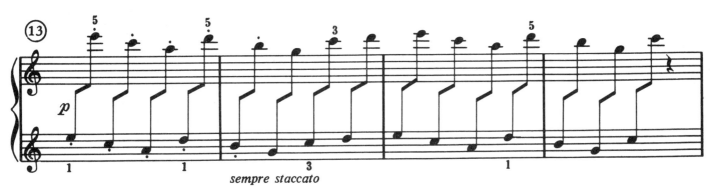

sempre staccato

Secondo

Primo

BOURRÉE

Secondo

JUNE WEYBRIGHT

BOURRÉE

Primo

JUNE WEYBRIGHT

REMINISCENCE

Secondo

MICHAEL AARON

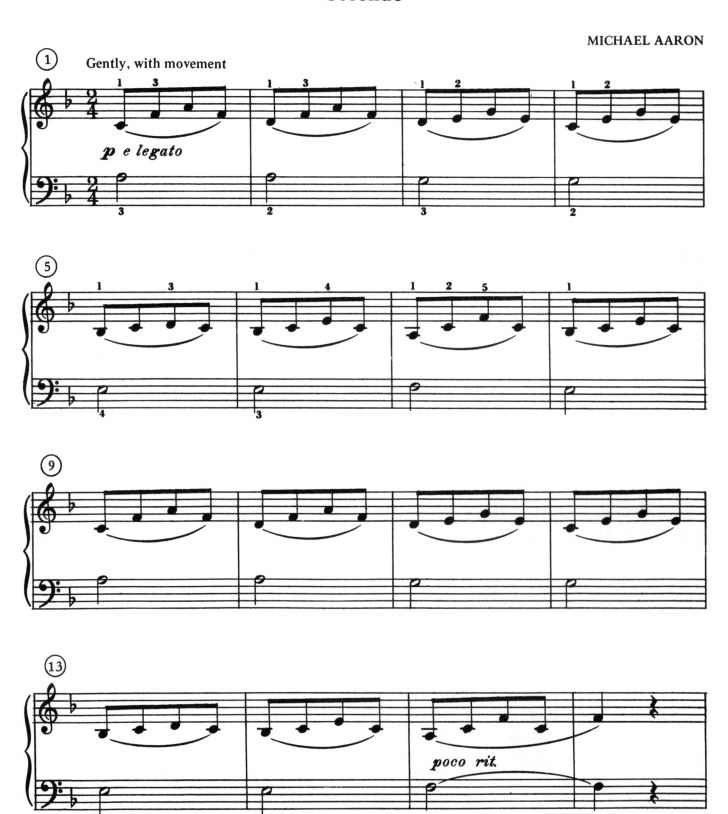

REMINISCENCE

Primo

MICHAEL AARON

Secondo

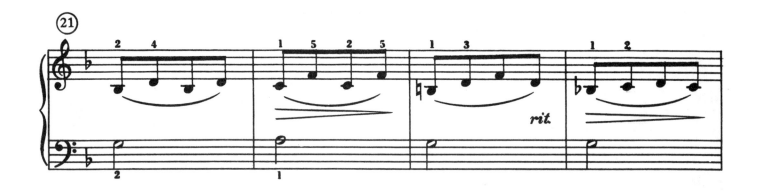

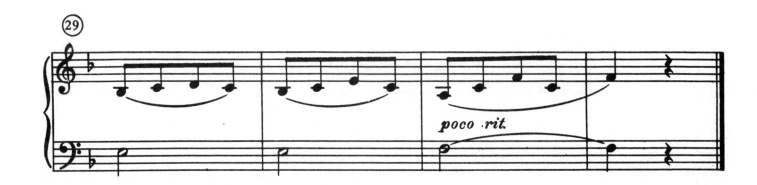

ANDANTE GRAZIOSO

Secondo

JON GEORGE

ANDANTE GRAZIOSO

Primo

JON GEORGE

EVENING NOCTURNE

Secondo

DAVID A. KARP

EVENING NOCTURNE

Primo

DAVID A. KARP

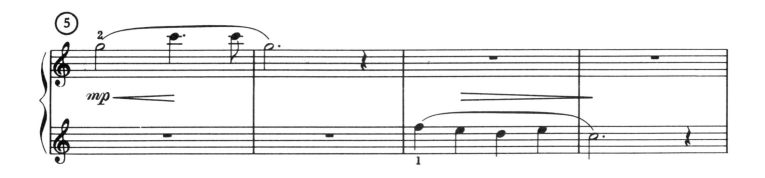

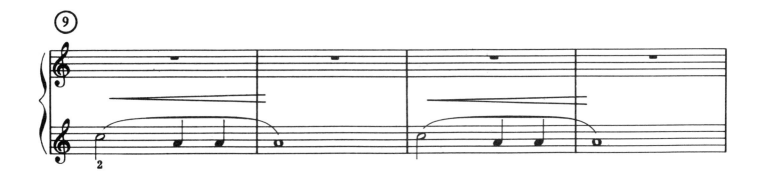

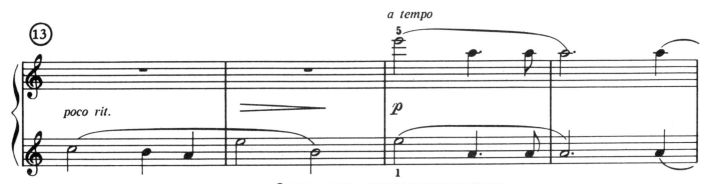

Secondo

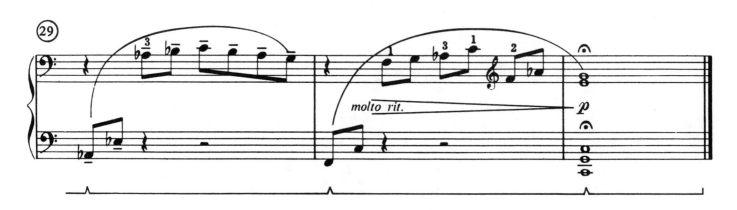

Primo

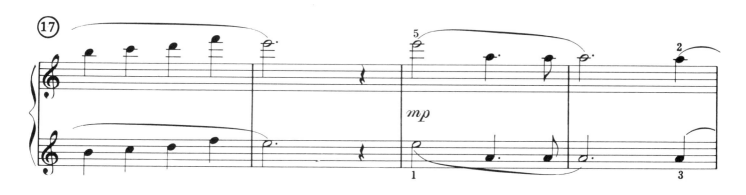

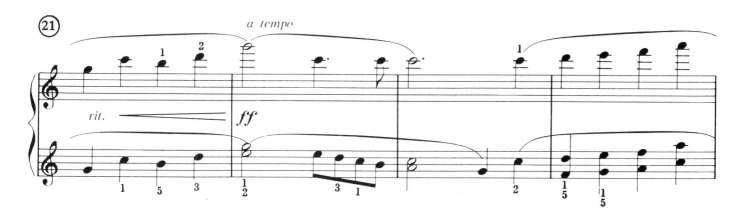

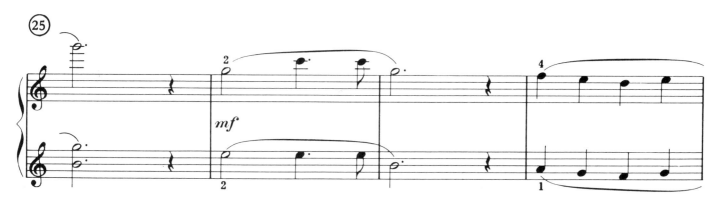

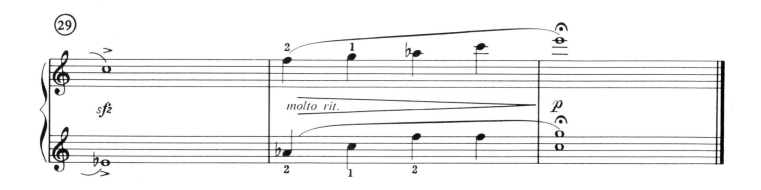

CLOWNS
Secondo

DAVID CARR GLOVER

CLOWNS

Primo

DAVID CARR GLOVER

Secondo

Primo

THE DANCING STARLET

Secondo

Rather quickly, with motion

JOHN W. SCHAUM

THE DANCING STARLET

Primo

JOHN W. SCHAUM

Secondo

Primo

THE CLOWN

Secondo

MICHAEL AARON

THE CLOWN

Primo

MICHAEL AARON

WALTZ SIMPLICE

Secondo

WALTER NOONA

WALTZ SIMPLICE

Primo

WALTER NOONA

Secondo

Primo